THE SHADOW OF MY SOUL. -MY INNER VOICE PART-1

A VERY SMALL COLLECTION OF POEMS

ADHYA. K . K

Made with ♥ on the Notion Press Platform
www.notionpress.com

To you beautiful souls...

Contents

Foreword

I flinched when I tried to talk it out;

So I wrote it down.

Preface

"The Shadow of My Soul" is a journey deep into the mind, dwelling into the finer things that make our lives so much more meaningful.

Acknowledgements

Thank you for choosing my book :)

Prologue

I wanna be me to the fullest.

1. As I am...

Today I talked to my body.
"Why does my waist have to be so cinched?
Why wouldn't these tummy roles disappear?
Why do I have all these stretch marks that I hate?
Why does almost everything about you
averse to the beauty standard?
Why are you like this despite everything
I do to make you look good?
What exactly do you need?"I asked her;
As I stood in this dark room
thinking about everything about her
that I wished was different
and waiting for her reply.
She whispered very gently
as her voice broke
"Could you love me as I am?"

-adhyakk

2. A daffodil in a dessert

Like a daffodil in a desert,
I had to grow in the cruelest conditions,
clasping on to every drop of rain,
just to stay alive;
For I wanna live,
before I die.
I wanna blossom
beneath this blazing sun,
show you all that I wanna become,
bring out all the colours
living inside of me,
and thrive despite all the hindrance I went through.
I wanna be me
to the fullest.

-adhyakk

3. Will you?

Will you break my trust,
forgetting every promise you ever made,
making it hard for me to trust again?
Will you strip away my self-worth
layer after layer,
ensuring that I let slip all that I am,
losing the ability
to love myself?
Will you put me through hell,
Causing me to feel so naive,
that I showed you I'd stay
through everything?
Will you beat me down to nothing,
Proving to me that hurting me never hurt you,
And bury me in your graveyard of lies?
Will you?

-adhyakk

ADHYA.K

4. A Ray of Light.

As the pale shadow of darkness
walked into her life,
she found herself drowning
in her own sea of sadness.
She was reduced to tears
as she stepped out of her chamber
with her mind filled with fear,
while her thoughts began to spiral.
As a ray of light fell on her face,
she peeped through the windows
to the rustic beauty of the rising sun
that brought her soul peace.
She quickly stepped out
to immerse herself in the beauty of nature.
The beautiful sky
with cottony clouds of feathery gold,
the melancholy of the early birds
and the delicate drizzles,
the soft whispers of the morning breeze,
the healing hues of a rainbow,
the beaming sunlight
that fell on the growing crops
and the radiant rivers,
where the world was mute

and her mind was calm
she found herself enchanted
to an ocean of opportunities
as she gained the courage
to vanquish yesterday's gloom.

-adhyakk

5. Until the day you took me home...

I was stuck in between
Like a growing bamboo
thinking about the way you make me feel everyday;
and how watching you walk into a room
would make my mind go astray.
How do I tell them
just how hard it is
to be with you in my dreams and wake up all alone,
wishing I was wrapped tight in your arms
for they really feel like home?
You crawl in my mind
when I try to sleep at night;
make me dream of being with you,
holding your hands real tight.
You make me feel things
in ways no one else can.
So I tell myself,
"I'll hold you in my heart
till I can hold you in my arms."
Hollow and wretched was how I felt,
until the day you took me home;
Now, how do I tell you
just how amazing it is,
to close my eyes,

listen to your voice
and know you're lying right here, next to me?

-adhyakk

6. The Baby You Never Had...

In your womb
I was slowly growing
hearing your endearing voice every single day.
Everytime you felt blue,
I felt it too.
I got everything I needed in here,
through you;
sensed myself flourish
and felt grateful to be yours,
for I thought you loved me so much
that you gave me this warm home within you.
But suddenly, I felt something strange intrude my home;
I couldn't breathe anymore.
The pain was too much to endure.
I cried out to you
and now here I am,
realising so many awful things at once!
I inhale fear,
now I know that you're gonna be both my joy and sorrow.
I was waiting to meet you on the other side;
to be held by your loving arms and be pampered.
Little did I know
that you wanted me dead,
for I always thought I was something you treasured.
I'm right here in you

with this beating heart of mine,
hoping I get to see you
and make it out alive;
yet I'll always be called
"the baby you never had".

-adhyakk

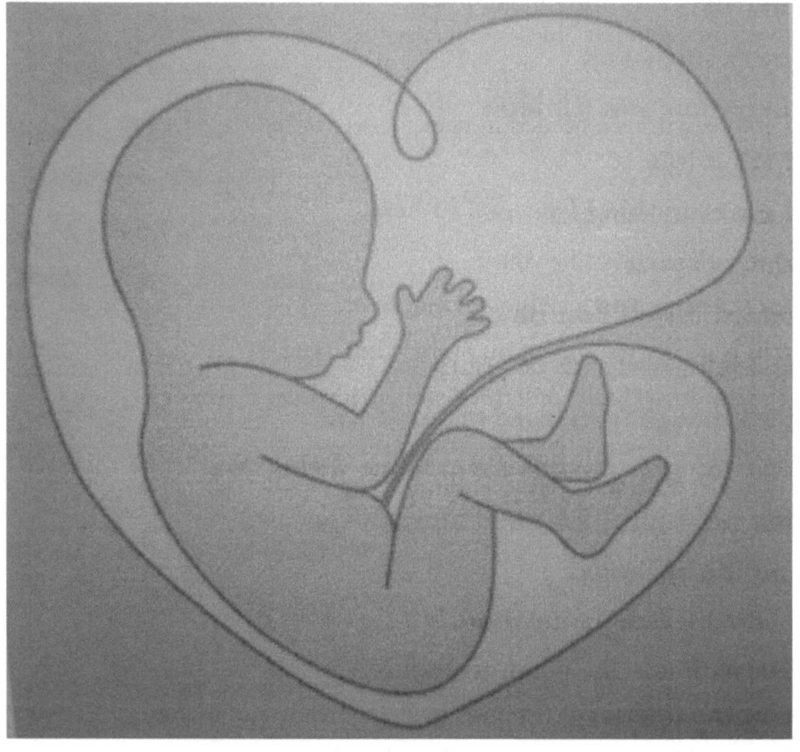

7. Gloomy days...

Too many times in the world today,
folks like us feel like we're being torn apart
and compelled to endure the gloomy days
when we feel like there's an eternal void
in our ephimeral souls,
for we feel so lost and low in infinite ways,
all at once.
When the bad outweighs the good
and emptiness feels too heavy to carry,
give your soul the rest it needs,
but, also feel what you need to feel
for even nature
needs to let it all out sometimes;
allow space for all the feelings your heart holds,
but when you do,
remember that there's much more to you
than the feeling you're not through
for the good things are still here.
Don't you give up now,
for it won't rain forever;
this journey's got twists and turns
but everytime you break remember that you only rise stronger.
So hang in there for a little more while
for you're gonna ace it in no time.

-adhyakk

About The Author

Hey there! I'm Adhya and I really enjoy writing.I seek to learn more and express my thoughts and ideas through my work and carve a niche for myself in people's beautiful minds.

Printed by Libri Plureos GmbH in Hamburg, Germany